ESTHER & RUTH

REFORMED EXPOSITORY BIBLE STUDIES

A Companion Series to the Reformed Expository Commentaries

Series Editors

Daniel M. Doriani
Iain M. Duguid
Richard D. Phillips
Philip Graham Ryken

ESTHER & RUTH

THE LORD DELIVERS
AND REDEEMS

A 13-LESSON STUDY

REFORMED EXPOSITORY
BIBLE STUDY

JON NIELSON
and **IAIN M. DUGUID**

P.O. BOX 817 • PHILLIPSBURG • NEW JERSEY 08865-0817

Scripture quotations are from the ESV® Bible (The Holy Bible, English Standard Version®), copyright © 2001 by Crossway, a publishing ministry of Good News Publishers. Used by permission. All rights reserved.

All boxed quotations are taken from Iain M. Duguid's *Esther & Ruth* in the Reformed Expository Commentary series. Page numbers in quotations refer to that source.

ISBN: 978-1-62995-758-6 (pbk)
ISBN: 978-1-62995-759-3 (ePub)
ISBN: 978-1-62995-760-9 (Mobi)

Printed in the United States of America

CONTENTS

SERIES INTRODUCTION

Studying the Bible will change your life. This is the consistent witness of Scripture and the experience of people all over the world, in every period of church history.

King David said, "The law of the LORD is perfect, reviving the soul; the testimony of the LORD is sure, making wise the simple; the precepts of the LORD are right, rejoicing the heart; the commandment of the LORD is pure, enlightening the eyes" (Ps. 19:7–8). So anyone who wants to be wiser and happier, and who wants to feel more alive, with a clearer perception of spiritual reality, should study the Scriptures.

Whether we study the Bible alone or with other Christians, it will change us from the inside out. The Reformed Expository Bible Studies provide tools for biblical transformation. Written as a companion to the Reformed Expository Commentary, this series of short books for personal or group study is designed to help people study the Bible for themselves, understand its message, and then apply its truths to daily life.

Each Bible study is introduced by a pastor-scholar who has written a full-length expository commentary on the same book of the Bible. The individual chapters start with the summary of a Bible passage, explaining **The Big Picture** of this portion of God's Word. Then the questions in **Getting Started** introduce one or two of the passage's main themes in ways that connect to life experience. These questions may be especially helpful for group leaders in generating lively conversation.

Understanding the Bible's message starts with seeing what is actually there, which is where **Observing the Text** comes in. Then the Bible study provides a longer and more in-depth set of questions entitled **Understanding the Text**. These questions carefully guide students through the entire passage, verse by verse or section by section.

It is important not to read a Bible passage in isolation, but to see it in the wider context of Scripture. So each Bible study includes two **Bible Connections** questions that invite readers to investigate passages from other places in Scripture—passages that add important background, offer valuable contrasts or comparisons, and especially connect the main passage to the person and work of Jesus Christ.

The next section is one of the most distinctive features of the Reformed Expository Bible Studies. The authors believe that the Bible teaches important doctrines of the Christian faith, and that reading biblical literature is enhanced when we know something about its underlying theology. The questions in **Theology Connections** identify some of these doctrines by bringing the Bible passage into conversation with creeds and confessions from the Reformed tradition, as well as with learned theologians of the church.

Our aim in all of this is to help ordinary Christians apply biblical truth to daily life. **Applying the Text** uses open-ended questions to get people thinking about sins that need to be confessed, attitudes that need to change, and areas of new obedience that need to come alive by the power and influence of the Holy Spirit. Finally, each study ends with a **Prayer Prompt** that invites Bible students to respond to what they are learning with petitions for God's help and words of praise and gratitude.

You will notice boxed quotations throughout the Bible study. These quotations come from one of the volumes in the Reformed Expository Commentary. Although the Bible study can stand alone and includes everything you need for a life-changing encounter with a book of the Bible, it is also intended to serve as a companion to a full commentary on the same biblical book. Reading the full commentary is especially useful for teachers who want to help their students answer the questions in the Bible study at a deeper level, as well as for students who wish to further enrich their own biblical understanding.

The people who worked together to produce this series of Bible studies have prayed that they will engage you more intimately with Scripture, producing the kind of spiritual transformation that only the Bible can bring.

Philip Graham Ryken
Coeditor of the Reformed Expository Commentary series

INTRODUCING ESTHER AND RUTH

ESTHER

The book of Esther is set during the reign of King Ahasuerus (also known as Xerxes)—the Persian ruler who reigned from 485–465 B.C. and is best known for his wars against the Greeks. The action thus takes place about fifty years after the decree of Cyrus, which allowed the Jews to return home from their exile in Babylon. Many of the most committed Jews did so, including Haggai, Zechariah, Ezra, and Nehemiah. Others opted not to be part of the rebuilding process—especially those who already had comfortable jobs and living situations in the heart of the Persian empire. They preferred comfortable assimilation to the foibles of the Persian empire over the hard path of obedience to the Lord's call to rebuild Jerusalem and its surroundings. One such family was that of Mordecai, a descendant of King Saul's family, and Esther, his orphaned cousin. She also had a Jewish name, Hadassah, but publicly went by her Persian alias. These two insignificant nobodies would never have dreamed that they might have a significant part to play in God's plans; they were just trying to get by in life, even if that meant compromise with the empire.

The **main purpose** of the book of Esther is to show that God is able to take care of his people, using these very imperfect human agents, while remaining hidden from direct view. In the book of Exodus, God's work is full of dramatic interventions that expose the emptiness of the Egyptian gods. There are great heroes like Moses and Aaron to lead the people and a trail of miracles to attest to God's presence with them. In the book of Esther, however, there are neither dramatic miracles nor great heroes—just apparently ordinary providence moving flawed and otherwise undistinguished people into exactly the right place at the right time to bring the empire into line and to secure the future of God's people, when it seemed certain they would be eliminated.

There are no obvious clues as to who the **author** of the book of Esther was. Nor do we know whether it was written immediately after the events it describes or sometime later. None of that affects the meaning of the book, either for its original readers or for contemporary audiences.

The main **theme** of God's sovereign ability to take care of his people, with or without their help, is highlighted by the central turning point of the narrative. This is not when Esther determines to go to the king to plead for her people. That happens at the end of chapter 4; yet the fate of her people becomes worse during chapter 5, which ends with Haman about to hang Mordecai on a tall spike. The turning point is the king's sleepless night at the beginning of chapter 6, during which he asks for a reading from the royal annals (a surprising choice, given the range of options that would have been available to him), followed by a passage being read that mentions Mordecai uncovering a plot against his life. The king (again surprisingly) discovers that nothing has been done to reward Mordecai, and he then asks Haman—who has come to court early to ask for permission to hang Mordecai—for advice on how to reward "the man whom the king delights to honor" (6:6). From there onward, the tide turns in favor of Esther, Mordecai, and the Jews—and against Haman. Were all these things merely a series of random events? Certainly not. Even though God's name is nowhere mentioned in the book, he proves once again his power to rescue his people, even by using compromised people like Mordecai and Esther, who had almost given up on being distinctively Jewish in favor of pursuing career advancement within the Persian empire.

Yet not all the threats to Israel's safety are removed at the end of the narrative. To be sure, Mordecai is now second only to Ahasuerus in the empire, in place of Haman. Yet the king himself—the one who carelessly sold the Jews to slaughter—remains in place. The taxes that had been remitted when Esther became queen (2:18) are reimposed in the end (10:1). There is much for Israel to be grateful for in their deliverance from Haman's evil plan for genocide—something that became celebrated annually at the feast of Purim. Yet this partial deliverance still leaves them watching and waiting for the far greater deliverance that God promised them, through the coming of his Messiah.

Outline

Introduction: The Fall and Rise of a Queen (1:1–2:23)
  The Fall of Queen Vashti (1:1–22)
  The Rise of Queen Esther (2:1–23)

The Threat (3:1–5:14)
  Haman's Plan to Kill the Jews (3:1–15)
  Mordecai Persuades Esther to Intercede with the King (4:1–17)
  Esther Approaches the King (5:1–8)
  Haman's Plan to Kill Mordecai (5:9–14)

Deliverance (6:1–9:19)
  The King's Sleepless Night (6:1–3)
  The King Honors Mordecai (6:4–14)
  Esther Requests the King to Save her People (7:1–7)
  Haman Is Executed (7:8–10)
  Mordecai's Plan to Deliver the Jews (8:1–14)
  The Jews Are Victorious (8:15–9:19)

Conclusion: Celebrating the Victory (9:20–10:3)
  The Feast of Purim Is Established (9:20–32)
  Mordecai Replaces Haman (10:1–3)

RUTH

The book of Ruth opens with a key time indicator: "In the days when the judges ruled" (1:1)—a time when everyone did whatever was right in his own eyes (Judg. 17:6; 18:1; 19:1; 21:25). It is not clear during what part of the period of the judges these events took place, but the famine with which the book opens would have been during one of Israel's periodic times of unfaithfulness and idolatry. The book ends with the genealogy of King David, who was Boaz and Ruth's great-grandson.

The **main purpose** of the book of Ruth is to demonstrate the Lord's covenant faithfulness (hesed) to his undeserving people—which often manifests itself in hidden and surprising ways. Naomi interpreted the death of her husband and sons in Moab as evidence of the Lord's hand of judgment upon her for the sin of leaving the promised land in search of greener pastures (Ruth 1:21). This was indeed an act of unbelief, which resulted in her sons illegitimately marrying Moabite women (1:4). Yet in her bitterness, Naomi underestimated God's grace. Her daughter-in-law, Ruth the Moabitess, insisted on coming back to Bethlehem with her, and she turned out to be the means whereby the Lord would meet Naomi's needs—both for food to eat and for offspring to carry on the family name. What must have seemed to Ruth and Naomi to be a sacrifice of Ruth's future turned out to be the opening of a new future for her as part of the Lord's people. Ruth went out to glean in order to provide food for the family, and the "random" field that she chose turned out to belong to Boaz—the man who would ultimately fulfill the role of family redeemer for Naomi and Ruth. The genealogy of David at the end of the book shows how the Lord worked through this individual story of tragedy and redemption to provide for his people's need of a king. Not only was Naomi's bitterness turned to joy, but Israel's need for a godly leader was also being provided—even though no one could have anticipated it at the time. Though the Lord's actions are, in the main, concealed within this book, there are two specific events attributed directly to him: providing food for his people (1:6) and conception for Ruth (4:13). In these ways, the Lord provided for all his people's needs.

What is more, Ruth's covenantal commitment to Naomi and to Naomi's God demonstrated that those who were not ethnic Israelites could still be incorporated into the people of God through faith. If Moabites who joined themselves to the Lord could be accepted, there was hope for other gentiles as well (Isa. 56:3–7).

It is not clear who the **author** was, or when the book was written. The genealogy at the end of the book, and its need to explain customs that had gone out of fashion (Ruth 4:7), requires a date during or later than the reign of King David (1011–971 B.C.); though it could have been written as late as after the exile, when the issue of whether gentiles could become part of the covenant community once again became pressing.

As for its **themes**, the book of Ruth essentially replicates the parable of the lost son (Luke 15:11–32), in two strands. The family of Elimelech, in search of fullness, wandered away from the land where the Lord had promised to bless his people. Contrary to their expectation, Naomi ended up empty and alone. The Lord took away everything from her—not as an act of harsh judgment but as a means of bringing her back home, where he delighted to replace her emptiness with a new fullness. Similarly, the book opens with the Lord's people experiencing a famine because of their idolatry, as happened regularly in the days of the judges. Yet through this judgment, the Lord ultimately provided a king to meet their need for leadership. We too have gone astray from the Lord and need to receive his grace and mercy. Because of his covenant faithfulness, he has provided in Jesus Christ the Redeemer we all need. Jesus is the true King toward whom the genealogy of David ultimately extends (Matt. 1:5–6, 16), and he is the Redeemer in whom his wandering people find rest. In him, the gentiles too are incorporated into the people of God by faith and are granted a place in the family of promise.

Outline

Elimelech and Naomi Seek Grain and Offspring Outside the Promised Land (1:1–5)

Naomi Returns to Bethlehem Empty, Without Grain or Offspring (1:6–22)

Naomi and Ruth Receive Grain through the Lord's Covenant Faithfulness (2:1–23)

Naomi and Ruth Seek Rest in the Home of a Redeemer (3:1–18)

Naomi and Ruth Receive Rest in the Home of a Redeemer (4:1–12)

Naomi and Ruth Receive Offspring through the Lord's Covenant Faithfulness (4:13–17)

Israel Receives a King through the Lord's Covenant Faithfulness (4:18–22)

Iain M. Duguid
Coeditor of the Reformed Expository Commentary series
Coeditor of the Reformed Expository Bible Study series
Author of *Esther & Ruth* (REC)

ESTHER

LESSON 1

STANDING FIRM
AGAINST THE EMPIRE

Esther 1:1–22

THE BIG PICTURE

Roughly fifty years before the events that are recorded for us in the book of Esther, many of the exiled Jewish people—especially the ones who were most zealous for Jerusalem and for worshiping at the temple—had returned following the decree of King Cyrus of Persia. As we see, though, not every Jew returned. There were many of God's people who continued to live out their days in the midst of the great "dispersion," scattered among the nations following the invasion and destruction of Israel (the Northern Kingdom) and Judah (the Southern Kingdom). The story of the book of Esther focuses on this community of God's people—Jewish exiles who were seeking to hold on to their ethnicity and distinctive worship of Yahweh in the midst of powerful (and sometimes hostile) governing authorities.

As you may already know, Esther is the only book in the biblical canon not to mention the name of God. However, the fingerprints of God's sovereign care and preservation of his people—even in the midst of their exilic dispersion—are all over this account. In this opening passage today, we will find the setting for the story. The great and powerful King Ahasuerus sits on the throne in Susa, the capital city of the empire of Persia. In the midst of great feasting, the merry (and intoxicated) king sends for Queen Vashti to come before his guests and him, in order to show off her beauty. Shockingly, the queen refuses, and the king is urged by his advisers to make an example of her. With the queen now banished, we begin to understand that God is opening the door for his sovereign and surprising work of bringing a Jewish queen to the throne of Persia for the sake of rescuing his people.

Read Esther 1:1–22.

GETTING STARTED

1. Can you think of some instances or occasions that have made you very aware that, as a Christian, you do not quite belong—in a town, a club, or a group? How were you tempted to respond? Why is this awareness difficult?

> at work. I fear I would not be
> accepted for my beliefs.
> Jack – materialistic society (dallas)
> Both responding by trying to fit in. It is difficult
> because we know we are called to higher living
> + to profess our faith.

2. How do Christians in your community tend to think and talk about the governing authorities? Are they critical, to the point of being disrespectful? Do you ever see allegiance to nation or country that seems to be stronger than allegiance to Jesus Christ?

> 2021 Riots – people value their own ideas
> + selfishness over what the Lord wants
> for us + our country.
> no respect for our leaders any more, only hate.

Ordinary Providence at Work, pg. 7

In the book of Esther . . . we see God working invisibly and behind the scenes. Here there are neither dramatic miracles nor great heroes, just apparently ordinary providence moving flawed and otherwise undistinguished people into exactly the right place at the right time to bring the empire into line and to establish God's purposes for his people.

OBSERVING THE TEXT

3. As you read through the first nine verses of this passage, what obser-
   vations do you make about the descriptions that are included? What
   does the narrator seem to want you to notice about King Ahasuerus
   and his great party?

   Materialistic, wealth

4. What are you learning about the kingdom of Persia as you read and
   study this passage? Why might it have been difficult for a faithful, God-
   fearing Jewish person to live in this kind of kingdom?

   *Seemed to only revolve around
   the king
   King is very selective*

5. How does the chapter end? What questions do we, as readers, have as
   we come to the end of chapter 1?

   *Queen Vashti is banned
   a royal decree for women to obey their
   husbands.
   How does Esther become*

UNDERSTANDING THE TEXT

6. What does Esther 1:1 tell us about the power of King Ahasuerus and
   the vastness of the Persian empire? How does this compare with the
   state of the nation of Israel during this period?

   *Huge! He ruled 120 provinces

   The people of Israel weren't united
   and they had no power.*

7. As you read through Esther 1:1–9, what does the narrator seem to emphasize? What seem to be the values and concerns of the king and his subjects? How does this contrast with the kingdom of Jesus Christ?

The King surrounded himself with beauty, wealth, + power

- In the bible, we see God constantly using the seemingly unimportant

8. What seems to be the motivation behind the request that King Ahasuerus makes of Queen Vashti (1:10–11)? Why might she have refused this request—despite the potential consequences?

Pride + power.

insecurities, anger that he had power over her.

9. How do the "wise men" of the king advise him to deal with the refusal of the queen, and why do they give him this advice (1:16–20)?

To ban her + make an example.

- The decree

10. As the chapter ends, how does King Ahasuerus demonstrate his immense power throughout his kingdom? How might the final verse (1:22) be ironically and subtly pointing to future events in the story of Esther?

His decree went to every household

He will not have control over Esther

A Display of Excess, pg. 8

We are meant to be impressed and awed by this display of excess—and a little revolted by its wastefulness. . . . Ahasuerus is the very picture of power and wealth, both of which are squandered on his own appetites.

11. Do you see any direct evidence of the hand of God in the events of this passage? Why might the absence of any mention by the narrator of God's name and God's work point to important lessons for God's people in Esther's day—and in our day?

we know God is always at work and he always has a plan, even if we don't see it. We don't need proof that he is at work.

BIBLE CONNECTIONS

12. In the years leading up to the events of the story of Esther, many of God's people had returned to the land of Israel to rebuild the walls and the temple in Jerusalem—we read their stories in the books of Ezra and Nehemiah. While God certainly was working in and through the returned exiles in Jerusalem, what does the book of Esther tell us about his work on behalf of his people wherever they live? Why is this so encouraging?

13. Proverbs 21:1 describes God's sovereign power over the highest rulers of the earth in beautifully poetic terms: "The king's heart is a stream of water in the hand of the LORD; he turns it wherever he will." What might God be doing in and through the heart of King Ahasuerus in this passage?

It seems that God has hardened his heart, just like he did Pharoah's. It shows God uses all people to further His kingdom.

THEOLOGY CONNECTIONS

14. Robert Shaw, writing about God's providence, declares, "God has the interests of his own people ever in view; he knows what is most conducive to their happiness; and he will make all things, whether prosperous or adverse, to co-operate in promoting their good (Rom. 8:28)."[1] Why is this truth about God's providence sometimes difficult for us to believe? How must we, as God's people, be comforted by God's providence?

    Its good to know that God is always in control + always has a plan. This is hard to see when it doesn't go according to our plan.

15. Question and answer 34 of the Heidelberg Catechism explain that we call Jesus our Lord "because He has redeemed us, body and soul, from all our sins, not with gold or silver, but with His precious blood, and has delivered us from all the power of the devil, and has made us His own possession." How does this selfless love of our King, Jesus, contrast with the selfish love of King Ahasuerus for his bride in Esther 1?

    God gave His own body for us + King Aha was giving his bride's. Everything God does is for us, Everything Aha does is for himself.

APPLYING THE TEXT

16. What should we be learning from the description of the decadence and selfishness that King Ahasuerus displayed in his reign, partying, and rash decisions? How is this passage urging us not to take even powerful global rulers too seriously?

    we are blessed beyond measure. More than we deserve.

---

1. Robert Shaw, *The Reformed Faith: An Exposition of the Westminster Confession of Faith* (1845; repr., Fearn, UK: Christian Focus, 2008), 114.

17. How is this passage calling us to remember the significance and reality of God's sovereignty—even in the context of seemingly meaningless political moves and decisions? Why must we intentionally remember God's providence in all the details of our world?

> we must intentionally remember God's providence in our messed up world or we would have no hope. we have to remember that God is always in control

18. In what ways can you discipline your own heart and mind to remain steadfast in your loyalty to King Jesus, rather than to the kingdoms and power of this world? How does Jesus Christ, the great King, treat his bride, the Church?

PRAYER PROMPT

As you close this time of study in Esther 1, spend some time praising God for his sovereign care and providence—even when you do not readily observe his hand. Thank him that he is always at work for the eternal good of his people, whom Jesus Christ died to redeem. Pray that God would help you to remember the deep, selfless love of your perfect Bridegroom, even as you live daily as an exile in a fallen world.

A Great and Gracious King, pg. 15

The Lord too is a great king whose decrees cannot be challenged or repealed . . . [but] God doesn't use people for his own purposes as if they were disposable commodities. Rather, he graciously invites them into a loving relationship with himself.

LESSON 2

BEAUTY AND THE BEAST

Esther 2:1–23

THE BIG PICTURE

Enough time passes after the banishment of Queen Vashti that King Ahasuerus, under the advisement of his wise men, decides that he will select a new queen. The strategy for this seems like something we might find today on reality television: there will be a competition . . . and all young, single, beautiful women throughout the kingdom will be invited to participate! While this does seem crass and shallow, God nevertheless clearly works through this beauty pageant to bring an unlikely queen to the throne of Persia. In Esther 2, we are introduced to a Jew named Mordecai and to his young and beautiful cousin Esther. They are unlikely heroes, indeed—especially because, at this point in the story, Esther seems to be quietly assimilating to all of the pagan practices of the Persian empire. Yet, as we will see, they both have integral roles in God's sovereign and gracious plan to preserve the lives of his people—even in the midst of the brutal and pagan kingdom of Persia. The chapter ends with Esther assuming the role of queen and with Mordecai discovering and foiling an assassination attempt against King Ahasuerus. As readers, we expect that both of these events will have great import as the narrative continues.

Read Esther 2:1–23.

GETTING STARTED

1. In what ways does your surrounding culture seek to assimilate people to its preferred values, norms, beliefs, or treasures? How do you tend to feel such pressure most poignantly in your life and context?

   Social media - beauty, materialism, human rights.

   Government through laws - assimilation N gay marriage, abortion.

2. How are we sometimes tempted to become frustrated with God regarding his *timing*? When have you struggled with unanswered prayers or unfulfilled dreams? How were you tempted to view God in the midst of those disappointments?

   Hurt's miscarriages. why did one have to endure snot?

   Grandmother's passing - Mom's best friend.

The Bitter Fruit of Sin Transformed, pg. 28
We see in this chapter more than just the bitter fruit of disobedience.
We also see God's ability to turn our disobedience—and the sour fruits
of our parents' sins—to his own glory and his people's good.

OBSERVING THE TEXT

3. Upon your initial reading and study of Esther 2, what do you observe (or not observe) about Esther's thoughts, motivations, and feelings? Why might the narrator choose to generally *not* tell us what Esther is feeling and thinking?

> • Esther continues to withhold information b/c she's obedient to Mordecai (not telling she's a Jew). Doesn't take her cosmetics. Shows humility. Point is how God used Esther— not how she felt about it.

4. How does the narrator point to Mordecai in this chapter as a character who will be very important as the story continues?

> • Keeps referencing him checking on Esther — shows he cares for her. Also is obedient to the king by notifying him of a potential assassination.

5. What evidence, if any, of personal faith and courage do you see on the part of Esther and Mordecai in this passage? Where do you see evidence of the sovereign hand and plan of God?

> • Courage Esther for waiting a year to see the king. Knowing the king had other wives. Courage for Mordecai to alert the king of an assassination.
>
> • God's plan working by making his people prominent figures in this outside kingdom.

A Choice between Two Worlds, pg. 21

[Esther] too, like all the exiles, had to live in two worlds. As her life unfolded, though, there would come a day when she would have to decide which of those two worlds defined her.

UNDERSTANDING THE TEXT

6. What is surprising or striking to you about the competition that is established as this passage opens (2:1–4)? What are the requirements of the participants in this competition? How does this continue to reveal the character of King Ahasuerus and the values of his empire?

   • Virgins preparing for six months to have sex with the King. Shows he values labor and women's bodies.

7. What do you notice about the way Mordecai is introduced to us (2:5–7)? What does the narrator seem to think is important for us, as readers, to notice? What challenges might a faithful Jew like Mordecai have faced as he lived in the midst of the Persian empire?

   • True Israelite who is a faithful and honorable person - took Esther for his own after her parent died. Outsider even when he was a captive.

8. How is the hidden hand of God evident in the "favor" that Esther quickly wins (2:9–15)? What effect does she have on those around her?

   • Many who people in a position of power and control. People loved & respected her as the queen.

9. Note the description of the king's response to Esther (2:16–18). How does the narrator describe his delight in her? In what ways does the king honor her? Why might Mordecai have counseled Esther to stay quiet about her Jewish heritage in the midst of all this?

   • Made her queen and gave her the highest place in the palace. Revealed she was Jewish - could have been killed or not gotten position.

10. Why might the narrator have chosen to include 2:21–23—this record of Mordecai's role in the foiled assassination plot? How might this play a role as the narrative continues?

handwritten response:
- winning the king's favor. Background unclear/unimportant. Continuing to be faithful.

11. What are you learning about the sovereignty of God as you study this passage? How does the kingdom of Jesus Christ (and his role as Bridegroom in it) clash with the values of King Ahasuerus and his kingdom, as revealed in this chapter?

handwritten response:
- God's always at work even making things happen for his people.
- Jesus cares about our souls and unselfishly died for us. King Aha cares about himself and wanted a better.

BIBLE CONNECTIONS

12. There are interesting parallels between Esther 2 and Daniel 1—particularly with regard to the immense favor that God grants to a member of his covenant people who is in the midst of exile in a pagan empire. Take a moment to read Daniel 1:8–21. What similarities do you find between that account and this one from Esther 2—particularly regarding the favor that Daniel and Esther both win with those who are supervising them? What is different between the two accounts?

handwritten response:
- Went against the grain - vegetables and riches.
- Both were captives but attained high positions in the kingdom. They had with the kings.
- Heritage a secret (Esther), Daniel's was known.
- Background, anger, and alone (Esther) - Daniel had other men.

13. In Romans 12:2, Paul issues this call to believers: "Do not be conformed to this world, but be transformed by the renewal of your mind." What evidence do you see in Esther 2 of the Jewish characters' conformity to the world around them? As Christians, what does the "renewing" of our minds look like in the midst of a sinful world and/or culture?

- kept heritage a secret in order to for M.
- are different - Esther has a different M mean the others, Christians to me surve.
-

THEOLOGY CONNECTIONS

14. The Westminster Confession of Faith (5.1) describes the providence of God in this way: "God, the great Creator of all things, does uphold, direct, dispose, and govern all creatures, actions, and things, from the greatest even to the least, by his most wise and holy providence, according to his infallible foreknowledge, and the free and immutable counsel of his own will." How should this truth about God's providence inform our reading of Esther 2? Why is it so difficult for us to remember this doctrine amid the messy details of our world today?

15. The great reformer Martin Luther wrote about the kind, loving, and gracious heart of God: "I know nothing of any other Christ than he whom the Father gave and who died for me and for my sins, and I know that he is not angry with me, but is kind and gracious to me; for he would not otherwise have had the heart to die for me and for my benefit."[1] How does this description of the gracious heart of God

---

1. August Nebe, *Luther as Spiritual Adviser*, trans. Charles A. Hay (Philadelphia, 1894), 180–81.

contrast with what we see of the heart of King Ahasuerus in Esther 2? What motivates the king of Persia, in contrast with our Savior?

APPLYING THE TEXT

16. Assuming that Mordecai and Esther's relatives had been given the opportunity to return to life and worship in Jerusalem in 538 B.C. (probably fifty years before the events of Esther 2), how might we think about their decision to *stay* in Susa? What temptations do you face today to assimilate to a sinful culture rather than to live boldly and sacrificially for Jesus?

17. How is this passage calling you to consider and intentionally remember the reality of the hidden providential hand of God—even in the messiness of life in a fallen world?

No Beauty in Us, pg. 31
What motivated Jesus in his pursuit of us? Certainly not our radiant beauty and sweet spirit! We had all gone astray like rebellious sheep. . . . Nevertheless, he loved us and gave himself for us.

18. In what ways do the events of this passage remind you, by contrast, of the gracious realities of the kingdom of God? How can Esther 2 remind you of the otherworldly beauty and grace of Jesus Christ and of his loving posture toward you?

PRAYER PROMPT

As you come to the end of Esther 2, it is good to acknowledge that this is a messy and complicated chapter. Mordecai and Esther seem to be fairly assimilated into the Persian empire—going with the flow and hiding their true identity and allegiance. It is good for us to ask God for courage to always stand boldly for Jesus, no matter the cost. But, even in the mess and the failure we see here, we remember that God is working providentially in the events of this chapter—particularly in the placement of Esther on the throne in Susa. We ought to praise the sovereign God who works for the good of his people in a messy and sinful world!

LESSON 3

MORDECAI MAKES A STAND

Esther 3:1–15

THE BIG PICTURE

Esther 3 introduces us to the first real conflict we have encountered so far in the narrative. The ambitious and insecure Haman enters the story. A descendant of Agag and the Amalekites, he is promoted above all the king's other officials; King Ahasuerus even makes a special command that all people of the kingdom should bow before Haman. Mordecai, however, perhaps for reasons that are related to his and Haman's family lineages, refuses this command and does not bow before him. As word of this failure to comply is brought to Haman, he forms a retaliatory plan that seems disproportionate to the offense: he will wipe out not only Mordecai but all other Jewish people in the kingdom of Persia. King Ahasuerus is easily persuaded by Haman (with the help of a large sum of money that is paid into the king's treasury), and the chapter ends with the edict concerning the Jews spreading and causing chaos throughout the kingdom, even as Haman and the king sit down to eat and drink. God's people are perilously close to extinction, as the reader waits to see how the hidden hand of God will respond.

Read Esther 3:1–15.

GETTING STARTED

1. In what ways have you seen other Christians stand boldly for God and his Word in your culture? When have you observed people taking stands over issues that you would consider to be peripheral, secondary, or minimally important?

2. How have you observed hostility toward Christianity, the Bible, or the gospel of Jesus Christ in your neighborhood, town, or country? In what ways can such hostility sometimes be hidden, veiled, or disguised in various ways?

OBSERVING THE TEXT

3. What new characters are introduced to us in this chapter? What details about them does the narrator point out to us?

Newfound Convictions?, pg. 36
Mordecai was not necessarily wrong to refuse to bow before Haman. But let's major on the majors. There were perhaps other places where Mordecai should have first started to exercise his newfound convictions.

4. How have both Mordecai and Esther assimilated to the kingdom and customs of Persia thus far in the narrative? Why should Mordecai's refusal to bow to Haman thus be somewhat surprising to us?

5. What does King Ahasuerus's role in this chapter seem to be? How is this similar to—and different from—what we have seen in the previous chapters of Esther thus far?

UNDERSTANDING THE TEXT

6. As the narrator describes the promotion of Haman (3:1), what does he include about Haman's family and lineage? Why might that be significant? Why might it be an important detail for understanding Mordecai's response to Haman? (See question 12 for more biblical context.)

7. Does the narrator give any indication as to whether Mordecai's refusal to bow to Haman is godly and noble or foolish and small? Why might that be? What conclusions can we draw about Mordecai from this chapter?

8. In what ways do Mordecai's peers respond to his refusal to bow to Haman? How and why does Haman's hostility expand from Mordecai to encompass to all of the Jewish people (3:5–6)? What does the narrator seem to want us to notice about the actions and character of Haman?

9. How is Haman able to manipulate King Ahasuerus into complying with his plan to destroy the Jews (3:8–11)? What lies does he tell, and how does he seek to motivate the king to make the decree?

10. Why might Esther 3:11—and the king's statement about the people belonging to Haman—be an ironic and humorous verse? What do we know about God, which Haman and King Ahasuerus ultimately do not know?

Satan's Ongoing Warfare, pg. 37

Haman's enmity toward God's people was merely the latest manifestation of Satan's ongoing warfare against the people of God. The struggle for the hearts and minds of mankind that began in the garden continues on throughout time and space, and those who belong to the people of God will frequently feel the assaults of the Evil One.

11. What is the stark contrast that is set up at the conclusion of this chapter (3:15)? How is the narrator continuing to show us the character of Haman and of King Ahasuerus? What questions are we left with at the close of Esther 3?

BIBLE CONNECTIONS

12. As you may remember, Mordecai is a Jew, and also a descendant of the family of King Saul. Haman is evidently related to Agag—former king of the Amalekites. Take a few moments to skim over 1 Samuel 15. How might the events of that chapter help us to understand the mindset of Mordecai, as he refuses to bow before Haman?

13. We have seen already the way that the story of Esther mirrors the story of Daniel, in terms of the noteworthy favor that both Jewish exiles gained in the eyes of pagan royal officials. Now again, in Esther 3, we find more echoes of the story of Daniel. Take a moment to read Daniel 3, noting particularly verses 17–18. What additional details are included in the Daniel account regarding the matter of refusing to bow or worship? What similarities do you find between Esther 3 and Daniel 3?

THEOLOGY CONNECTIONS

14. Historically, the Reformed tradition has strongly affirmed the legitimacy of political rulers and civil governments. According to the Westminster Confession of Faith, "God, the supreme Lord and King of all the world, hath ordained civil magistrates to be under him over the people, for his own glory, and the public good: and, to this end, hath armed them with the power of the sword, for the defense and encouragement of them that are good, and for the punishment of evildoers" (23.1). How, though, are Haman and King Ahasuerus so obviously departing from God's intention for human governments through their actions in Esther 3?

15. In his famous *Institutes of the Christian Religion*, John Calvin wrote that we may be "content with this one thing: that our King [Jesus] will never leave us destitute, but will provide for our needs until, our warfare ended, we are called to triumph" (2.15.4). Why is this an encouraging picture of our King Jesus—especially when contrasted with King Ahasuerus?

Edict of Destruction, pg. 42
The edict for our destruction could legitimately have been signed against us by our Great King. But that is not how God, the true sovereign King, has chosen to deal with us.

APPLYING THE TEXT

16. As you consider the stand that Mordecai takes against bowing to Haman, how are you challenged to stand more boldly for God and his Word in your daily life? In what ways have you been guilty of standing boldly for peripheral issues while failing to stand courageously for core gospel concerns?

17. What ought this part of Esther—and particularly the interaction between Haman and King Ahasuerus—remind us about the futility of putting our ultimate trust in politics or political leaders? With what mindset and realizations ought we to engage politics in our world?

18. As Esther 3 draws to a close, a callous and careless king sits down to drink as thousands of vulnerable Jews in his kingdom come under a death warrant. How should we view his behavior in this scene as a stark contrast to the actions of our Savior and King, Jesus Christ? In what ways is King Ahasuerus continuing to serve as a foil to the true King?

PRAYER PROMPT

As you consider Esther 3 and its place in this ongoing narrative, begin asking God today for the courage and boldness to stand for him in the midst of hostility, disdain, and even suffering. While we do not know Mordecai's exact motivation for refusing to bow to Haman, we know our own call to worship and serve God alone. Pray that God would give you the strength, grace, and wisdom to thoughtfully and humbly engage your neighbors and friends with the good news of the gospel of Jesus Christ, the King who offers himself in the place of his needy and helpless people.

LESSON 4

THE DOG THAT DIDN'T BARK

Esther 4:1–17

THE BIG PICTURE

As Esther 3 ended, King Ahasuerus and Haman were sitting down to drink as the rest of the kingdom was thrown into confusion. An edict had gone out that sentenced the dispersed Jewish people of the Persian empire to execution. As the next chapter starts, though, there is one Jewish person who seems to be completely oblivious to the imminent danger and chaos—Queen Esther sits secure in the palace, known only as "Queen" Esther and not as Esther the "Jew." This does not last long, though; Esther hears that her cousin Mordecai is publicly mourning and draped with sackcloth. He refuses her attempts to bring him clothing and comfort and ultimately makes a huge request of Esther: to go before the king and appeal to him to deliver the Jewish people from their death sentence. Esther initially balks; to go unsummoned before King Ahasuerus could mean punishment—even death. But, as Mordecai appeals to her by pointing out that she may well have been strategically placed "for such a time as this," she invites the prayers of her Jewish kinsmen and prepares to take her life in her hands before King Ahasuerus. This chapter comes closest to recognizing the hand of God; there is a deeper purpose behind this Jewish queen, and it has to do with the salvation of God's people.

Read Esther 4:1–17.

GETTING STARTED

1. How have you been aware of times when God's hidden hand has placed you—or someone else—in exactly the right place at exactly the right time? In what ways did that grow your faith and trust in God?

2. Have you ever been faced with a choice between the "easy way out" and the right, but more difficult, option? How did you weigh your options? How did God factor into your decision?

Unseen, Unheard, Unrecognized, pgs. 45–46

In a sense, the whole book of Esther is similarly about the one character who never appears on stage, never speaks, and is never actually spoken to: God. Nowhere is that more true than in chapter 4, where Esther must place her life in the hands of the unseen, unheard, and unrecognized God.

OBSERVING THE TEXT

3. As the passage opens, how is it immediately evident that Esther is isolated and insulated from both the Jewish community and the threat of danger?

4. Glance through Mordecai's impassioned appeals to Esther in this chapter. What points does Mordecai raise? How does he ground his words to Esther? What is surprisingly absent in his speeches to her?

5. Consider all that Esther has to lose if she does what Mordecai asks. What truths and realities seem to begin to change her mind as the chapter goes on?

UNDERSTANDING THE TEXT

6. As the passage opens, how are the Jewish people responding to the announcement that has just been circulated throughout the kingdom (4:3)? What is missing from their response? What might that tell you about the spiritual state of many of the Jews who were living in Persia?

7. What does Esther 4:4–8 tell us about Esther's awareness of the decree of the king? How does she seek to comfort Mordecai? What might that attempt at comfort reveal about her initial understanding of the imminent danger that is faced by the Jewish people?

8. What do you make of Esther's initial response to Mordecai's request of her (4:9–11)? What seems to worry Esther, as she considers going before the king to make an appeal?

9. Mordecai's words of earnest appeal to Esther are well known to students of the Bible (4:12–14). How would Esther have heard and understood those words from Mordecai? What is Mordecai implying about a purpose and plan behind Esther's rise to a royal position? How does this moment point us to God's hand in the story, even though he is not mentioned by name?

Undercover Believer, pg. 51

Esther now had a clear and life-changing choice to make. She could no longer live in the blurred shadows of two worlds. Up until now, she had been living as an undercover believer. . . . To continue to do so was no longer possible.

10. Consider the choice Esther now has before her. What might her fears be? What additional challenge and perspective has Mordecai set before her?

11. What is noteworthy about Esther's request regarding the Jews in 4:16? How is this different from the behavior we have seen from Esther in the past? What do her final words in the chapter reveal about her heart and intentions (4:17)?

BIBLE CONNECTIONS

12. Even though Esther goes somewhat reluctantly before King Ahasuerus to plead for the lives of the Jewish people, her decision to take her life in her hands does point forward to a far better Mediator—one who pleads for God's people with his own blood. Take a moment to read Matthew 26:37–39. Note Jesus's struggle before going to the cross. How does the struggle of Esther 4 anticipate this far greater cosmic struggle?

13. As we have seen before, the story of Esther can remind us that followers of God should expect hostility from a pagan world. Read Jesus's words in John 15:18–25. How should these words influence our expectations for life, and our expectations for others' acceptance, as we live for Jesus in this world?

THEOLOGY CONNECTIONS

14. The New City Catechism counsels us to pray "in humble submission to God's will, knowing that, for the sake of Christ, he always hears our prayers."[1] Why might prayer have been missing in the account we are studying from Esther 4? How could prayer have been helpful for both Mordecai and Esther?

15. Esther 4 concludes with Esther deciding to step forward to serve as a mediator on behalf of the Jewish people. The great reformer Martin Luther once penned these words: "The sinner needs a better mediator. That better mediator is Jesus Christ. He does not change the voice of the Law, nor does He hide the Law with a veil. He takes the full blast of the wrath of the Law and fulfills its demands most meticulously."[2]

---

1. *The New City Catechism: 52 Questions and Answers for Our Hearts and Minds* (Wheaton, IL: Crossway, 2017), answer 39.

2. Martin Luther, commentary on Galatians 3:20, in *A Commentary on St. Paul's Epistle to the Galatians*, trans. Theodore Graebner (Grand Rapids: Zondervan, 1949).

How should this passage from Esther fill our hearts with thankfulness for our better Mediator?

APPLYING THE TEXT

16. If there were any time for the Jews throughout Persia to cry out to God for mercy and help, it was in Esther 4! Yet, even in the midst of the mourning and fasting and weeping, we see no mention of prayer. When have you been guilty of prayerlessness, even as you endured difficult times? How can you avoid prayerlessness in the future?

17. Esther, secure in the palace as queen, faced no imminent danger, as her Jewish identity was unknown. How might she have been tempted to respond? How are we often tempted to care only for our own comfort and safety rather than for that of others?

The Plight of God's People, pg. 56

Esther's actions raise serious questions for each of us to answer. Am I still blind to the true nature of the world and the plight of many of God's people around me? Do I know enough about what is going on in the world to mourn and lament the situation of God's persecuted people?

18. Mordecai's challenge to Esther is one that we each should make to ourselves: we ought to consider where we have been strategically placed, according to God's plan, and how we might best serve the purposes of our Savior and his gospel. How might you more intentionally do that in your own current placement?

PRAYER PROMPT

As you close your study of Esther 4, and of this difficult choice placed before Esther, spend some time asking God to open up your heart to have compassion for, and to lament over, the plight of God's people who are in danger or in need or who face persecution. Ask him to help you to remember the global church—your brothers and sisters in Christ. Pray that God would make you bold to stand for gospel truth . . . and ask him to deepen your trust in a Mediator who is far greater than Esther—one who stands at the very right hand of God.

LESSON 5

MEEKNESS AND SUBTLETY

Esther 5:1–14

THE BIG PICTURE

Esther 4 has left us, as readers, with a heavy moment of tension. Esther has listened to Mordecai's appeal and decided to mediate between her Jewish people and the king. She knows that approaching the king means taking her very life in her hands, yet she has resolved to go anyway (4:16). Now, Esther 5 quickly shows us the king extending his scepter to Queen Esther; she has won favor in his sight, and he invites her to make any request of him—up to half of his kingdom. Esther, though, acts slowly, carefully, and subtly. She invites both King Ahasuerus and Haman to an exclusive feast, where again the king invites her to make a request. Instead, Esther requests their presence at yet another feast. Haman goes away gleefully—giddy over his privileged position in the presence of the king and queen. But his glee quickly turns to rage as one man, Mordecai the Jew, still refuses to give him adulation and honor. The chapter ends with Haman erecting a huge gallows, on which he intends to hang Mordecai. As careful readers, we know that the unseen and silent God is very much at work—bringing every detail into place to execute both salvation for his people and judgment on their enemies.

Read Esther 5:1–14.

GETTING STARTED

1. When have you felt called to directly engage or challenge something that was unbiblical, unjust, or antithetical to God's Word? How have you sometimes sought to bear witness to Jesus in more subtle, quiet ways?

2. Why can it be difficult for us to trust the sovereign plan of God when he is so often unseen, quiet, and mysterious? What might the Jews of Esther's day have been wondering about God's plan for them and presence with them?

The Careful Fisher, pg. 63

Esther was playing the king like a trophy fish, taking her time and not rushing to reel him into her net. She was carefully maneuvering him into a position where he would be virtually obligated to do whatever she asked, without his even being aware that he had been hooked.

OBSERVING THE TEXT

3. How would you characterize the actions and words of Esther throughout this passage? Why might she be acting so slowly, carefully, and methodically throughout this chapter as she works her way toward making a big request to King Ahasuerus?

4. What additional information do we gain about Haman in this chapter? How are his character flaws and personal idols further revealed through both his elation and his anger?

5. Consider the way Esther 5 concludes. What questions are we left with? How is the narrator artfully telling the story?

UNDERSTANDING THE TEXT

6. How do the opening verses of this chapter (vv. 1–2) offer us resolution to the tension we felt as chapter 4 ended (note Esther's words in 4:16)? In what way is this a hopeful moment—one that reminds us of God's hidden hand in Esther's life?

7. What might Esther be seeking to accomplish by delaying her actual request to King Ahasuerus? Why would she include Haman in this special feast with the king?

8. What do Haman's joy and gladness in the first part of 5:9 reveal to us about his motivation, values, and treasure? What does his wrath in the rest of that verse reveal to us about his character and deepest idols?

9. What counsel would you have given to Haman, following his comments to his friends and wife (5:11–13)? What dangerous tendencies do you see in his boasting and his complaint?

10. How would you evaluate the advice that is given to Haman by his wife and friends (5:14)? Why might this advice be so pleasing to Haman?

Subtle Work, pg. 68
Notice that God's plan in this case was worked out without thunder and lightning, or a parting of the sea in order to save his people. . . . God's work here is every bit as subtle as Esther's.

11. While God is (again) not mentioned in this chapter, he is certainly using every moment described in this passage—from Esther's words to Haman's anger—to set up salvation for his people. Where do you notice glimpses of God's careful arrangement and sovereign plans throughout this chapter?

BIBLE CONNECTIONS

12. The apostle Peter offers some words of guidance to Christian women who are married to men who are not walking closely with the Lord.

    > Likewise, wives, be subject to your own husbands, so that
    > even if some do not obey the word, they may be won with-
    > out a word by the conduct of their wives, when they see
    > your respectful and pure conduct. (1 Peter 3:1–2)

    How does Esther demonstrate respectful and pure behavior and conversation to her husband, the king? Why is this so effective?

13. Read the wonderfully encouraging statement that Hebrews 4:16 makes. How, as Christians, can our approach to the throne of God be different from Esther's approach to the throne of King Ahasuerus? Where must our confidence be grounded?

THEOLOGY CONNECTIONS

14. God acts sovereignly over his world in a way that does not diminish real human responsibility. According to the Westminster Confession of Faith, "Although in relation to the foreknowledge and decree of God, the first cause, all things come to pass immutably and infallibly, yet, by the same providence, he orders them to fall out according to the nature of second causes, either necessarily, freely, or contingently" (5.2). How might you explain both "first causes" and "secondary causes" using Esther 5? Consider the relation between God's sovereignty and the real decisions and actions of Esther, King Ahasuerus, and Haman.

15. The Scots Confession, written largely by the Scottish reformer John Knox, summarizes Jesus's role as Mediator for us with these words: "He, being the clean and innocent Lamb of God, was damned in the presence of an earthly judge, that we should be absolved before the tribunal seat of our God" (chap. 9). How does Esther's favor before the king paint a picture for us of our ultimate and eternal favor before the throne of God?

APPLYING THE TEXT

16. As this chapter begins, we as readers breathe a deep sigh of relief—King Ahasuerus extends his scepter to Esther and grants her access to his presence. How ought this to give us a small glimpse of the privilege of the access we ourselves have been granted to the holy presence of

God, through the grace of Jesus Christ? How can we better celebrate and appreciate that privilege?

17. As we see the ugly, self-consumed heart of Haman being revealed to us in this passage, it is healthy for us to consider our own temptations toward idolatry. How might God be calling you to destroy the idol of acceptance and praise by others? How might he be calling you to accept criticism from others with more humility and grace?

18. How can Esther's careful, precise, and meek approach to her relationships and her conversations with the king inform the way that we, as Christians, can engage the world around us with wisdom? How can we evaluate when to directly engage something and when to carefully, quietly, and subtlety bear witness?

Free but Not Cheap, pg. 70
Our entry to the heavenly court is free, but it was not cheaply bought. As sinners, a death is required before we can enter the presence of the all-holy One. God can hold out the golden scepter of favor to us only because the fierce rod of his judgment has fallen upon Christ.

PRAYER PROMPT

Esther 5 paints a picture of a careful, meek, humble woman who artfully sets up a political ruler for a difficult request. All the while, even in the midst of intentional human action, we know that God is quietly working for the preservation and deliverance of his people. Today, spend some time asking God to remind you of his absolute sovereignty, even as you seek to intentionally, carefully, and wisely obey him according to his Word. Then thank him that, as sovereign King of the universe, he grants access and favor to you, and praise him that you can draw near to him through the blood of Jesus.

LESSON 6

THE MAN THE KING DELIGHTS TO HONOR

Esther 6:1–14

THE BIG PICTURE

As we came to the end of Esther 5, the tension continued to mount. The Jewish people's lives still hang in the balance because of the edict of death that has been issued against them. Esther has succeeded in putting on a feast for King Ahasuerus and Haman, but she has not yet interceded forcefully for her people. Now, in addition, we know that Mordecai's life is in danger—even more imminently than the lives of the Jewish people are. Haman has gone out to erect a giant pole on which to hang Mordecai's body. Amazingly (and humorously!), in the midst of this tension, we find a seemingly random turn of events. In the midst of a sleepless night, King Ahasuerus commands that the chronicles of his reign be read to him, and he hears the account of Mordecai's discovery and exposure of the plot against his life—an action that is yet to be publicly acknowledged and rewarded. As if by chance, Haman is nearby, and the king calls him for his counsel regarding how to rightly honor a valued servant. Haman's ego leads him to immediately assume that he is this man, but his plan is ironically turned upside down when he is forced to publicly heap honor and adulation on the one man he hates most: Mordecai. Even Haman's own family cannot ignore the signs now that he is fighting a hopeless battle against Mordecai, as he is whisked away to the second feast with Esther. Here, again, we trace the quiet, hidden hand of God, as he takes the plans of his enemies and turns them on their heads . . . just as he does ultimately at the cross of his own Son.

Read Esther 6:1–14.

GETTING STARTED

1. Have you ever observed a malicious plan brutally and ironically back-firing on the person who orchestrated it? Can you think of examples of this in great literature, stories, or films? Why is this so enjoyable to observe?

2. You are about to study a passage that hinges, at least in part, on a seemingly random bout with insomnia. How have you seen very small, seemingly insignificant, events or occurrences play a big part in God's overall plan in your own life? In the lives of others?

The Perfect Case Study, pg. 74

Between the lines and behind the scenes, out of focus and incognito, the Lord continued to work to accomplish all his holy will. Esther 6 is a perfect case study in God's way of working all things together for the good of his people.

OBSERVING THE TEXT

3. Based upon your initial reading of this passage, how would you summarize the way that this chapter continues to develop the character of King Ahasuerus? What continues to be revealed about the character and motivations of Haman?

4. What evidences do you see of God's hidden sovereignty and providence in this passage, even as he continues to remain unmentioned?

5. Consider the way that this chapter closes. What seems to be significant about the words of Haman's family? What may the narrator be trying to help us to notice and understand?

UNDERSTANDING THE TEXT

6. As the passage opens, what hints do we have that God is quietly and secretly at work (6:1–2)? How is this similar to glimpses we have seen of the hidden hand of God earlier in the story?

7. What might be motivating King Ahasuerus's desire to honor Mordecai (6:3)? How is his behavior in this chapter consistent with what we have observed about him so far?

8. Haman immediately assumes that King Ahasuerus delights to honor *him* (6:6). Why might he be assuming this, based on earlier details in the narrative? How does this assumption—as well as the manner of exaltation that he suggests—show us Haman's heart?

9. What are we told about Haman's response to being forced to honor Mordecai in this way (6:12)? Why are we, as readers, so delighted by this ironic reversal? How might Haman have an opportunity, even in this moment, to repent and change his heart toward Mordecai—and toward God?

Unwilling Declaration, pg. 84
Haman unwillingly declared Mordecai's honor. He was forced to declare his praise. So also some will unwillingly declare the honor of Christ on the last day. . . . How can we not exalt Christ in our hearts as Lord, even now?

10. In some ways, the words of Haman's wise men and of his wife come the closest in the entire book to pointing to God's hand in this story (6:13). What do they tell Haman about his experience with Mordecai? How do they relate it to the role of the Jewish people?

11. What warnings should we take from this passage, as we observe the actions and words of Haman? How does Esther 6 point us forward to the gospel of Jesus Christ—and particularly to his final and ultimate exaltation?

BIBLE CONNECTIONS

12. In Esther 6, Haman discovers—much to his ultimate chagrin—that there is a man whom the king delights to honor. That man is *not* him— instead, he will have no choice but to share in bestowing honor on Mordecai. Take a moment to read Philippians 2:10–11. How does this point to a greater man whom God delights to honor? What choice will the world have as far as bestowing ultimate honor on Jesus at his return and exaltation?

13. Read Acts 5:34–40, which describes the advice that Gamaliel gives to the Jewish leaders concerning the apostles. How are Gamaliel's words similar to what Haman's wise men and family told him? What principles do both Gamaliel and Haman's friends affirm?

THEOLOGY CONNECTIONS

14. There are plenty of occurrences in Scripture of God acting in extraordinary, miraculous, and visible ways. But far more often in Scripture—and in our lives as well—God acts quietly, ordering all things according to his will. In Reformed doctrine and thought, this quiet, sovereign work of God is often referred to as his "ordinary providence," which refers to the way God accomplishes his eternal purposes in the midst of very ordinary events. What are some ways that this "ordinary providence" of God is evident in Esther 6?

15. Martin Luther once quipped that "the best way to drive out the devil . . . is to jeer and flout him, for he cannot bear scorn."[1] How do we see the enemies of God's people being mocked in this passage—and being unable to bear scorn?

---

1. Quoted in Alexander Chalmers, "Life of Luther: Memoir," in *The Table Talk of Martin Luther*, trans. and ed. William Hazlitt, new ed. (London, 1857), lxxxvi.

APPLYING THE TEXT

16. How can you more actively and consistently trust God's providential work in your life—even when you can't see it? What truths about the character of God that emerge from this passage of Esther should you more intentionally remember?

17. As we continue to get to know Haman, his idolatry and sinful motivations are exposed more and more. What can you learn from his obsession with attention, flattery, and self-exaltation? How can you repent and turn from an obsession with self and from the idolatrous need to be praised?

18. In this great ironic reversal—the exaltation of the very man whom Haman desires to execute—we see a glorious and humorous picture of the cross of Jesus Christ. How can this passage teach you about the beauty and irony of the work of Christ? In what ways should Esther 6 drive you toward worship of your God?

The Trees Tell Their Own Story, pg. 79
As we look outside through a window, we can neither see nor feel the wind blowing, but the bending of the trees tells its own story. So too, here in the book of Esther, God's work of providence is so clear that even the pagans cannot miss its significance.

PRAYER PROMPT

As we have been seeing in our study of Esther, the hand of God is so often hidden from sight—and yet it is active in the midst of seemingly small, random, and insignificant details in our lives. God is always at work—even in the tossings and turnings of a pagan king in Persia! Today, thank God for his hidden, steady, sovereign hand, which is working out all things for the eternal good of his people. Praise him for confounding Satan's plan to destroy Jesus, just as he confounded Haman's plan to destroy the Jews. The greatest degradation—the cross of Jesus Christ—became the path toward the eternal exaltation of our Lord and Savior.

LESSON 7

COMING OUT IN SUSA

Esther 7:1–10

THE BIG PICTURE

The moment has now come. Esther has gathered King Ahasuerus and Haman for yet another evening of feasting—this will be the big reveal. Queen Esther, living safely in the palace of the king, has never before revealed her Jewishness—even from the beginning she has been fully plunged into the Persian lifestyle, customs, and culture. By this point, King Ahasuerus has already publicly promised to grant Esther whatever her request may be—even up to half his kingdom (and he reaffirms this declaration as our chapter opens). The time is right; Esther makes her move. She reveals to the king that she and her people have been "sold"—not as slaves, but into destruction and execution (7:4). As the anger of King Ahasuerus is quickly kindled, Esther points out Haman as the culprit. The king—furious, and yet surely puzzled over how he will reverse an unbreakable edict—momentarily exits the room. When he returns, he finds a scene that clinches Haman's fate, as well as giving him the excuse he needs to execute Haman: Haman begs for his life before Esther, falling inappropriately onto her during his distressed plea. In a dramatic turn, Haman is impaled on the very pole that he had constructed for Mordecai's execution! So the enemy has been defeated . . . but the edict against the Jews still stands, leaving the reader waiting to see the full deliverance of God.

Read Esther 7:1–10.

GETTING STARTED

1. How have you experienced the interplay between God's sovereignty and human responsibility in your life? When have you felt called to act decisively in order to make something happen? How do you trace God's sovereignty as you look backward at events in your past?

2. In what contexts are you most tempted to keep your faith in Jesus quiet, hidden, or secret? Why might this be?

Esther Outs Herself, pg. 86
Now it was time for Esther to come out of the closet. Haman's edict threatened the whole Jewish community and, for the sake of her people, she had agreed to go before the king to intercede with him for their lives. That was going to be a tricky proposition, for King Ahasuerus was a dangerously unstable individual.

OBSERVING THE TEXT

3. Look back for a moment at the end of chapter 6. How did the words of Haman's friends and family prepare us for the events of chapter 7? In what ways did this incident point to God's hidden hand at work?

4. What do you notice about Esther's words and tone as she speaks to King Ahasuerus in this passage? How does she demonstrate careful and artful persuasion throughout the chapter?

5. How does Esther 7 further develop our understanding of King Ahasuerus—his character, personality, and motivation? In what ways should we be continuing to contrast him with King Jesus?

UNDERSTANDING THE TEXT

6. What does King Ahasuerus again affirm in 7:2? How does this continue to build Esther's confidence and credibility as she prepares to make her request?

7. How does Esther describe the plot of Haman against the Jews (7:3–4)? What do you notice about the words she chooses? What does she choose not to include?

8. In what way does Esther climactically call out Haman (7:6)? What is Haman's immediate response?

9. Why might King Ahasuerus have walked out to the garden (7:7)? What dilemma did this King of Persia now face, given his queen's recent revelation?

10. How does Haman ultimately seal his fate (7:8)? Does King Ahasuerus really believe that Haman has attempted to assault Queen Esther? If not, how might the king be using this situation to his benefit?

The Ticking Time Bomb, pgs. 90–91

Even though Haman personally had been dealt with, his edict still remained out there, like a ticking time bomb, just waiting to explode and destroy the Jews. Esther herself might be safe, guarded within the king's palace, but that wasn't what she had gone through this whole routine to achieve.

11. What surprising and ironic reversal occurs as this chapter concludes (7:10)? How is this a picture of the ironic reversal of the gospel and the cross of Jesus Christ? What question still remains (and whose lives hang in the balance) as this chapter ends?

BIBLE CONNECTIONS

12. Take a moment to read Genesis 12:1–3—God's original promise of blessing to Abram. How do you see God's promises being fulfilled here in Esther 7—particularly through the downfall of Haman, who has certainly been guilty of "cursing" God's people?

13. As Jesus died on the cross, many people mocked him and thought him publicly "shamed." But read Colossians 2:15. What does Paul say that Jesus, on the cross, actually did to the evil and demonic enemies of God? How do the events of Esther 7—and particularly the nature of Haman's death—point us to the beautiful irony of the shame of the cross?

THEOLOGY CONNECTIONS

14. In question 11 of the Heidelberg Catechism, God's wrath and justice are affirmed: "God is indeed merciful, but He is also just; therefore His justice requires that sin which is committed against the most high majesty of God, be also punished with extreme, that is, with everlasting punishment of body and soul." In what ways does Haman's sad demise remind us of the reality of God's wrath and judgment against sin?

15. The Reformed tradition upholds the grand doctrine of the sovereignty of God, but not without also affirming real human responsibility. How do you see human responsibility functioning in Esther 7—particularly in the unfolding plan and actions of Queen Esther? In what ways is it evident that the sovereign hand of God is ruling over the events of this chapter as well?

APPLYING THE TEXT

16. For years, Esther had kept her Jewish identity hidden in the midst of the pagan, Persian empire. Are there ways in which you hide your identity in Christ? How might God be calling you to reveal more boldly your love for Jesus and your commitment to his Word?

17. While we believe in the sovereignty of God, we as God's people are often called to decisively and obediently act—just as Esther acted boldly in this chapter we have been studying. In what ways might the doctrine of God's sovereignty be used as an excuse for human inaction in matters of obedience and witness?

18. King Ahasuerus continues to be revealed to us as a man who is fickle, easily swayed, and out to preserve his own image and reputation. How does this contrast with your King and Savior, Jesus Christ? What do you need to remember about Jesus, by way of contrast with this Persian king?

The Only Truth That Will Last, pg. 95

God's people are those who have built their lives around the only truth that will last, the truth of a King who is utterly different from Ahasuerus. We have a King who doesn't need to be manipulated and cajoled to do what is right. Our King does what is right because he himself is righteous—he cannot do anything other than the right.

PRAYER PROMPT

Esther 7 shows us a woman boldly taking action—identifying herself with the people of God and interceding for them on the king's behalf. As you close your study in Esther today, ask God for the courage and boldness to reject both sinful inaction and inappropriate secrecy about your faith in Jesus. Pray that he would embolden you to identify yourself with Christ, even in the midst of a hostile world. Thank him for his sovereignty, which should encourage you to live faithfully and obediently as you follow a crucified and risen Savior. Finally, praise him that he is a King who does what is right, without needing to be manipulated or convinced!

LESSON 8

IT AIN'T OVER

Esther 8:1–17

THE BIG PICTURE

Haman, the great enemy of God's people, has been put to death. Esther's life, at least, is safe. And, as chapter 8 begins, we see Esther and Mordecai being richly rewarded by King Ahasuerus, with Mordecai taking over the full estate of Haman (8:1–2). Yet the edict of the king commanding the destruction of the Jews still stands. So Esther approaches the king with a second request—this one much more direct—as she tearfully pleads for the reversal of the deathly edict against her people. King Ahasuerus initially responds simply by reminding Esther of what he has already done: he has executed Haman and transferred his property and position to Mordecai. But ultimately the king grants an important allowance to the Jewish people, as he permits them to gather, organize, and defend themselves against any attacking enemy force (8:9–14). As the chapter ends with the Jewish people preparing to make their "holy war" on their enemies throughout the kingdom of Persia, we are left with a violent reminder that God's plan and will must not be opposed. The hand of God, which has been moving silently and secretly throughout the story of Esther, will now bring down fierce vengeance on all who oppose his people.

Read Esther 8:1–17.

GETTING STARTED

1. In what ways have you been tempted to care only about your own comfort and welfare rather than caring about that of others? What tends to encourage and inspire you to sacrifice for others, even if it involves damage to your own comfort and safety?

2. How have you struggled with the reality of God's justice, his judgment of sin, or the doctrine of hell? What lies at the root of those struggles? How have you sought to explain these doctrines to others who struggle with them?

A New Perspective, pg. 102

Even though Esther had once concealed her identity because her only thought was to protect herself, now that she had identified with her people, she had a new perspective that stretched beyond her own narrow self-interests. Salvation for herself was not enough if it came without salvation for her people.

OBSERVING THE TEXT

3. Look at Esther's demeanor before King Ahasuerus in the first verses of this chapter. How has she changed from the way we saw her in earlier chapters? What do you notice about her apparent heart for her people, the Jews?

4. In what ways have Mordecai's appearance and demeanor changed in this chapter? How might this be an indication that the condition of God's people in Persia has changed overall?

5. How does the chapter conclude—especially for the Jewish people throughout the kingdom of Persia? Describe the drastic shift in their attitudes from what we saw a couple of chapters earlier in the narrative.

UNDERSTANDING THE TEXT

6. How do the people of God continue to receive favor from King Ahasuerus as the chapter begins (8:1–2)? In what ways might we understand even this as the fulfillment of God's promises to his people?

7. Describe Esther's approach, tone, and strategy as she makes this second appeal to the king (8:3–6). How is this different from her carefully planned first appeal? Why might this be?

8. How does King Ahasuerus seem to initially respond to Esther's request (8:7)? What might he be implying to her about what he has already done for Mordecai and her?

9. While the edict prepared by Haman is not exactly overturned, a second edict is quickly circulated throughout the kingdom (8:9–14). What is the content of this edict? Why is it so significant for the Jewish people throughout the kingdom?

Holy War, pg. 107

What, then, is holy war? In holy war, the Israelites acted as the agents of God's righteous judgment against sinners. . . . They functioned as a kind of human equivalent to the fire and brimstone from heaven that destroyed Sodom and Gomorrah . . . or the flood of Noah's day, which wiped out an entire generation of humanity.

10. How do the Jews respond to the letters that are sent out throughout the kingdom of Persia? What is the response of the non-Jewish people in the kingdom? How does this teach us about the sovereign plan of God and his love for his people?

11. What is difficult for us, as Christians today, as we consider the militaristic approach of Mordecai and the Jews in this passage? How might this passage be calling us to better understand the seriousness of sin and the reality of God's wrath and judgment?

BIBLE CONNECTIONS

12. Read 1 Samuel 15:1–3, noting God's command to King Saul to completely wipe out the Amalekites, along with their king. What does this command teach us about the justice of God and the seriousness of sin? How does it connect to the themes of this chapter of Esther?

13. Hebrews 9:11–15 presents Jesus Christ as the great "mediator" between sinners and a holy God. Read those verses now. How has Esther served as a lesser picture of the glorious mediation of Jesus Christ, the Savior?

THEOLOGY CONNECTIONS

14. The Westminster Confession of Faith states, "God in his ordinary providence maketh use of means, yet is free to work without, above, and against them, at his pleasure" (5.3). How do we see God clearly making use of "means" (natural events, human choices, and so on) in this chapter of the Book of Esther?

15. R.C. Sproul, while writing on the wrath of God, remarked, "The most violent expression of God's wrath and justice is seen in the Cross. If ever a person had room to complain of injustice, it was Jesus. He was the only innocent man ever to be punished by God. If we stagger at the wrath of God, let us stagger at the Cross."[1] Why is it so important to remember the cross of Jesus Christ in the midst of discussions about violent expressions of God's judgment in the Old Testament?

---

1. R.C. Sproul, *The Holiness of God*, 2nd ed. (Carol Stream, IL: Tyndale, 1998), 121.

APPLYING THE TEXT

16. Earlier we saw Haman pleading for his own life. Now, in Esther 8, Queen Esther tearfully intercedes before the king for the lives of her people. How can this serve as an example for us? How can it encourage us by presenting a picture of our Savior?

17. While we as God's people today are not called to take up instruments of war against enemies of the gospel, we are called to boldly proclaim Jesus and to defend the faith. In what ways might this chapter inspire us to courageously join together for the sake of the gospel?

18. Esther 8 ends with great joy among the Jewish people . . . and with fear of the Jews falling on all other people (8:17). When faced with the reality of God's wrath against sin and his coming judgment, how are we called to respond? How must God's judgment be included in our proclamation of the gospel of Jesus Christ?

An Esther of Our Own, pg. 109

Who will deliver us from the edict of death that still stands against us in the heavenly court? What we need is an Esther of our own, someone who will put aside personal interests and safety and risk dignity, honor, even life itself, in order to plead our case before God, the Great King.

PRAYER PROMPT

Esther's tearful intercession before King Ahasuerus in this chapter is a glorious picture of our Savior, who intercedes for us before the throne of God through the power of his blood. Today, praise your Savior again for his powerful intercession on your behalf! Then spend some time praying about your own bold witness for Jesus Christ and for his gospel in your community. Consider, prayerfully, how you might better partner with others in order to make him known. Ask God to help you to remember his grace, as well as the reality of his coming judgment, as you spread the good news of his salvation through Jesus.

LESSON 9

A WORLD TURNED UPSIDE DOWN

Esther 9:1–10:3

THE BIG PICTURE

The very first verse of Esther 9 offers a good summary of the conclusion of this grand story: "On the very day when the enemies of the Jews hoped to gain mastery over them, the reverse occurred: the Jews gained mastery over those who hated them." This is, indeed, the final word of the book of Esther—this great reversal that God brings about for the sake of the preservation of his people in the kingdom of Persia. Haman's plan is foiled; the Jews are preserved; their enemies lie slain by the thousands; Mordecai and Esther are exalted to positions of power and authority under the king. The slaughter is massive: 75,000 of the enemies of the Jews are killed throughout the king's provinces (9:16). This causes even King Ahasuerus to call out in amazement and offer to grant even *more* requests for Esther (9:12)! So Haman's sons are hanged, putting an even more decisive end to the family of this enemy of the Jews. Finally, in the midst of this massive victorious moment, the feast of *Purim* is inaugurated—it is established to commemorate this amazing deliverance and victory for the Jewish people (9:26). The book concludes with a further elevation of Mordecai, as well as with Esther holding an authoritative role in the distribution of letters throughout the kingdom. Even so, some of the final words of the narrator describe a new tax that is levied on the people by King Ahasuerus. We are reminded that a pagan king still sits on the throne and rules over God's dispersed and exiled people. They will still need a better King—an ultimate Redeemer.

Read Esther 9:1–10:3.

GETTING STARTED

1. What are some of the most surprising and ironic reversals you can think of—in history, politics, or athletics? What is inspiring about such stories?

2. How have you seen people struggle with the violence of Old Testament passages—particularly ones in which God's people are commanded to annihilate their enemies? What are some of the best answers you have heard to questions about this?

The More Things Change . . . , pg. 121
The more things change, the more they stay the same in the empire of Ahasuerus. [We should notice] the extent of the reversal that has happened for the Jews. Yes, the Jews have received rest from their enemies all around . . . except for one enemy, Ahasuerus himself.

OBSERVING THE TEXT

3. The sheer violence of this passage can be a bit overwhelming for today's reader. What was your immediate response to reading these final two chapters of Esther? What surprises you? What makes you uncomfortable?

4. How do Esther and Mordecai continue to rise up in power and influence as the book concludes? Why is this good news for the Jewish people who are living in the kingdom of Persia? How is this evidence of God's sovereign hand and his care for his people?

5. What indications are there in this passage that this deliverance for the Jews is not their final and ultimate deliverance? Who still remains in political control of the Jewish people?

UNDERSTANDING THE TEXT

6. How does 9:1 summarize this chapter, as well as the entire book of Esther? In what ways does this reversal show us the sovereignty and character of God?

7. What do you notice about this victory of the Jews as it is described for us (9:2–10)? What details does the narrator choose to include, and why might they be significant?

8. How does King Ahasuerus respond to what is going on in his kingdom (9:12)? What is his response to Queen Esther? How does she seize the opportunity of the moment?

9. In what way is this great victory celebrated and commemorated (9:17–19; 29–32)? Who establishes this feast? How is this different from the way other Old Testament feasts and celebrations were initially established?

10. What is the response of the Jews to this great day of reversals? Do you see evidence of praise and worship being directed to God? Explain your answer.

11. As the book of Esther concludes, what positive results for the people of God are specifically noted (10:1–3)? What are indications, in chapter 10, that his people have not yet received ultimate freedom and deliverance from their enemies? How does the ending of the book of Esther point us toward the need for a greater King and Redeemer?

BIBLE CONNECTIONS

12. Read Ephesians 2:1–3. How are human beings described, apart from the work of Christ? How does this impact the way we understand the enemies of God's people from Esther 9?

13. Read 2 Corinthians 5:21. We have discussed Esther's mediation for the Jewish people as being a picture of Christ's mediation for us. How

does this verse from 2 Corinthians show us an even deeper aspect of the work Christ performed on our behalf?

THEOLOGY CONNECTIONS

14. Question 37 of the Heidelberg Catechism explains that Christ "bore, in body and soul, the wrath of God against the sin of the whole human race, in order that by His passion, as the only atoning sacrifice, He might redeem our body and soul from everlasting damnation." Why is this so encouraging—especially in light of the picture of God's temporal wrath (through the Jews) that we see in Esther 9?

15. While there is some debate within the Christian church about how Sabbath principles are to be applied to the Lord's Day, almost all Christians agree on the importance of setting aside the Lord's Day for corporate worship with God's people. How can the celebration of the feast of Purim, and the intentional, joyful remembrance of God's deliverance, inform and encourage our worship of God with his people each week?

A Deliverance Yet to Come, pg. 122
The feast of Purim, when properly understood, is more than just a reminder to God's people of his past ability to intervene decisively even while remaining hidden to all but the eye of faith. It also pointed beyond itself to show us the need for a greater deliverance yet to come.

APPLYING THE TEXT

16. As we see God bringing about a massive, ironic reversal in favor of his people, how might you be called to respond to what you are learning about him? What do you need to be reminded of with regard to God's character, goodness, or sovereignty?

17. It is obvious from these chapters that part of the reason why the book of Esther was written was to explain the meaning of the feast of Purim for the Jewish people. How can this book help us to better celebrate our Christian "feasts" today—mainly Christmas and Easter? What must we do to rightly remember the biblical reasons for these celebrations?

18. The "holy war" that the Jewish people wage against their enemies in Esther 9 serves as a vivid picture of God's fierce judgment against his enemies. How must we apply this passage to the fact that we, in our sins, are naturally "enemies" of God? How must this passage drive us toward the cross—and to the need for God's mercy and grace through Jesus?

Holy War and the Cross, pg. 123
In Christ, former Amalekites and Jews are now brought together into the glorious peace that flows to the one new people of God. Yet our peace has a great cost. Peace was established for us by God by declaring holy war on his own Son. This is what was happening on the cross.

PRAYER PROMPT

As we come to the end of the book of Esther, we should be astounded at the shocking reversal that has taken place. The entirety of the Jewish people throughout the kingdom of Persia stood under a sentence of death, while a man who hated them held the ear of the king. Now, Haman is dead and the enemies of the Jews have been slaughtered throughout the kingdom. We ought to spend time praising God for his faithful provision and marvelous care for his people. Do that now, in prayer! But spend some time humbly confessing sin to God, as well. If not for his grace in Jesus, we would stand guilty and condemned—subject to his fierce wrath and judgment. Pray, today, with thanksgiving in your heart for the cross of Jesus Christ.

LESSON 10

GRACE AT THE BOTTOM OF THE BARREL

Ruth 1:1–22

THE BIG PICTURE

The first verse of the book of Ruth makes clear that its events occur in the time when the "judges ruled" (1:1). There is no king in Israel; it is an era of rising and falling leaders, disorganized worship, and fickle faithfulness from the people of God. Even so, the story of Ruth shouts of God's grace, as he provides redemption to a broken and bitter woman—which points beautifully to the ultimate redemption of all of God's people through King David's greater Son.

As the story of Ruth begins, an Israelite named Elimelech has made the ill-fated (and perhaps faithless) decision to move his family to Moab during a time of famine. His sons both take Moabite wives after having sojourned in Moab for some time. Before long, though, Elimelech and both his sons have died, leaving Naomi widowed—along with her two Moabite daughters-in-law (1:5). As the famine in Israel recedes, Naomi decides to return home—insisting emphatically that Ruth and Orpah remain in Moab and seek out husbands there. Orpah takes her advice; shockingly, however, Ruth the Moabite clings to Naomi and refuses to leave her. With her well-known words of commitment and faith, she pledges herself to Naomi, her people, and her God. Naomi, bitter and angry with God, says nothing in response to Ruth and returns home, replacing her old name with one that means "bitter" (1:20). Yet, as the two widows return to Bethlehem at the beginning of the barley harvest, God's grace will enter into this broken and bitter story.

Read Ruth 1:1–22.

GETTING STARTED

1. When have you observed hardship, difficulty, or even tragedy coming as a direct result of people's foolish choices? What is your immediate, natural response when you see this happen? Why?

2. Why can bitterness so easily grip our hearts in the midst of grief, pain, and suffering? How have you seen God's grace surprise and heal people who are wrapped in bitterness and anger?

The X Factor, pg. 130

There is a mysterious X factor that is evident in the book of Ruth—a variable that has the power to change everything. It is the grace of God, which directs the outcomes of those decisions and events according to his sovereignty and good purpose for his people. . . . Ultimately, for Christians, the grace of God is always the defining element of our lives.

OBSERVING THE TEXT

3. Notice how much of Naomi's story is summarized, so briefly, in the opening six verses of Ruth 1. How would you describe Naomi's life up to this point? What would you be feeling if you were her?

4. What do you observe about the conversation between Naomi and her Moabite daughters-in-law? What points does Naomi make, and in what tone does she make them? What seems to be different about Ruth compared to Orpah?

5. Ruth 1 opens with a downward spiral into tragedy, grief, and pain. How does the chapter end with at least a glimmer of hope?

UNDERSTANDING THE TEXT

6. How might Ruth 1:1 provide not only a historical setting for the story of Ruth but also a theological setting for these events? Why might the intentional mention of the "judges" ruling be so significant for our understanding of this account?

7. While the narrator does not comment on the morality of Elimelech's decision to move his family to Moab, what might we assume about this choice (1:2)? Why might that have been a dangerous, if not even sinful, move for Elimelech to make?

8. Even after the death of her husband, Naomi would have been well cared for with her two sons still alive. Why would their deaths, then, have been such a crushing blow for her (1:5)? What seems to awaken in her a desire to return to the land of Israel?

9. Why does Naomi so forcefully oppose the idea of Ruth and Orpah returning with her to Bethlehem (1:6–13)? What other difficulties might they face in the land of Israel, given their Moabite ethnicity?

A Foolish First Resort, pgs. 148–49

Whether it is closed doors in our career path, financial difficulties, or shattered relationships, our first resort is often to blame God's harshness for our pain. The result of that attitude in our hearts may be that our lives become filled with such bitterness that we completely miss the providential marks of God's continuing goodness to us in the midst of our difficulties.

10. What do you notice about Ruth's impassioned speech to Naomi? What commitments does she make? What does she affirm? Is there evidence, in her words, of genuine faith in God? What is surprising about Naomi's response to Ruth (or her lack thereof)?

11. As the chapter ends, why might the narrator have included the detail about the beginning of the "barley harvest" (1:22)? How is this a hint that God is not yet finished with Naomi? How is this detail a reminder of God's grace to his people—both then and now?

BIBLE CONNECTIONS

12. Read Judges 2:16–20, which gives an overall summary of what has been called the "Judges Cycle." What do you notice about the pattern that is described here? Why is it important to understand this historical and theological backdrop of the story of Ruth?

13. In spite of Naomi's bitterness, God is at work bringing a Moabite woman, Ruth, to the land of Israel and to faith in him. This is a glorious picture of God's salvation making its way to the nations of the world. Read

Psalm 67 now. How does it celebrate the praise of God coming from the peoples and nations of the earth?

THEOLOGY CONNECTIONS

14. The Westminster Confession of Faith affirms that true believers in God can fall, for a time, under God's "fatherly displeasure" due to sin and disobedience (11.5). How might this shape the way we view Elimelech's sojourn in Moab as well as Naomi's angry bitterness?

15. In the Reformed tradition, the doctrine of "unconditional election" affirms that God, in his sovereignty, elects some for salvation, without basing that election on any merit, goodness, or earned favor in them. How do we see this doctrine being demonstrated in the amazing, faith-filled declaration of Ruth the Moabite (in contrast with the actions of her sister-in-law, Orpah)? How is her "conversion" evidence of God's sovereign grace and call?

APPLYING THE TEXT

16. Even after a sojourn in Moab, Naomi's return to Israel is a turn back to God's people, to God's place, and ultimately to God himself. How can

this return be seen as a hopeful picture of repentance? In what ways could this help you to encourage others to seek God, even after they have strayed toward sin and unbelief?

17. Ruth's speech to Naomi includes an amazing, difficult commitment to both her mother-in-law and the God of Israel. How might her words remind you of the commitments that you are called to make—to God, to your spouse, to the people of God, and to the gospel of Jesus Christ?

18. Naomi's words upon her return to Israel reveal a heart full of bitterness, grief, and most likely anger toward God. What truths about God that are found in his Word can protect you against this kind of bitterness when you experience suffering and grief?

The Passion of Ruth, pg. 152

It is deeply convicting that in Ruth it is the former pagan who has more passion for Israel's God than has the child of the covenant, who heard of his dealings with his people from her earliest days.

PRAYER PROMPT

The story of Naomi's life—at least up to the end of Ruth 1—is a devastating one. Death and tragedy surround her; suffering embitters her and hardens her heart toward God. Today, spend time praying that God would protect you from the hardening bitterness of sin—even when suffering comes. Then, ask God to help you to see again the beauty of his grace to you in Jesus Christ. You have a Savior who has made an even deeper and more eternal commitment to you than the one Ruth made to Naomi. Praise him for his faithfulness today.

LESSON 11

A REFUGE FROM THE STORM

Ruth 2:1–23

THE BIG PICTURE

Ruth 1 presented to us, rather quickly, the dramatic collapse of Naomi's fortunes. She had gone out from Israel to Moab full, with a husband and two healthy sons. And she had returned empty—full of bitterness and anger at a God who had seemingly abandoned her. Yet, as we saw, chapter 1 ended with a glimmer of hope: Naomi and Ruth returned to Bethlehem at the beginning of the barley harvest. Also, Naomi does not return alone—her Moabite companion has sworn her allegiance to her . . . and to her God as well.

Now, as chapter 2 opens, we find Ruth quickly taking the initiative—offering to go and "glean" in the fields in order to provide food for Naomi and herself. It just so happens that she comes to the field of Boaz, who is a relative of Naomi's dead husband, Elimelech. From Boaz's first words, which bless his workers with the name of Yahweh, we can see that he is a godly man. Boaz notices Ruth—and has already heard about her great kindness and loyalty to Naomi. He makes special concessions for her, instructing his men to specifically look after her as she gleans. Ruth returns, with a bundle of grain, to an amazed Naomi, who instructs her to stay close to this godly man and his field. As readers, we are beginning to see the grace of God powerfully breaking into the lives of Ruth and Naomi. God leads Ruth to the field of Boaz, and he will yet bring redemption to this story.

Read Ruth 2:1–23.

GETTING STARTED

1. The right timing is so important (as we will see in this chapter of Ruth!). Can you point to a time in your life—or in the life of a friend or relative—when God brought something about with perfect, sovereign timing?

2. Talk about a time when you have been surprised, or perhaps even overwhelmed, by God's goodness and faithfulness to you. How did this serve to soften your heart toward God and to root out bitterness?

From Emptiness to Fullness, pg. 156

There was food once again in Bethlehem. God's hand of judgment had been lifted from his people. Now if that trajectory from emptiness to fullness was possible for Naomi's people, perhaps her own future was not as dark as she imagined it to be. Even if God's face was turned aside from her at present, as she thought, perhaps his favor could yet be restored to her.

OBSERVING THE TEXT

3. Upon your initial reading of Ruth 2, what jumps out to you about the man Boaz? What do you notice about his words? How does he treat the people around him?

4. What do you notice, in this chapter, about the changing words and demeanor of Naomi? Why might she be slowly changing in these ways?

5. How does Ruth demonstrate both humility and decisive action in this chapter? Why is this balance so important, given her situation?

UNDERSTANDING THE TEXT

6. How does Ruth take initiative as this chapter begins (2:1–2)? What does Naomi's response tell us about her demeanor perhaps changing toward Ruth? How does her response here contrast with her response (or her lack thereof) to Ruth's impassioned speech in chapter 1?

7. The narrator's literal words, in Hebrew, tell us that Ruth came to Boaz's field "as if by chance" (2:3). Why might this be a tongue-in-cheek comment from the narrator? How should we understand this "coincidence" in light of the sovereign plan of God?

8. What do Boaz's first words in the narrative tell us about his character (2:4)? What might the narrator want us to notice in particular about this man?

9. How does Boaz's initial conversation with Ruth further develop and reveal his character and integrity (2:8–12)? What is surprising about his words to Ruth—especially considering her ethnicity? Why is this particularly striking during the period of the judges?

10. What has Boaz obviously heard about Ruth already? What special commands does he give to his men concerning her (2:15–16)?

A Means of God's Goodness, pg. 163

The reference to Boaz as redeemer, moreover, points our eyes beyond him to the figure of the Redeemer. The . . . grammatical ambiguity [in Ruth 2:20] over whether it was Boaz or the Lord who was showing favor to Ruth and Naomi was profound rather than accidental. Boaz was the means that God used in a small way to show Naomi his goodness.

11. How does Naomi respond to Ruth's day of gleaning (2:18)? What instructions does she give to Ruth when Boaz's identity is revealed to her (2:19–22)? What hints are we getting as to Naomi's softening heart? What does she say about God? What are *we* learning about God through his goodness and grace in this chapter?

BIBLE CONNECTIONS

12. Read Leviticus 19:9–10 and Deuteronomy 24:19–20. How do these passages provide helpful context for what Naomi sends Ruth out to do at the beginning of this chapter (2:1–2)? What do these instructions from God's law teach us about the character of God and his concern for the poor?

13. Naomi's words to Ruth in 2:20 identify Boaz as a "redeemer"—a kinsman who may offer protection and provision to a close relative. How does this reference—and even this word—point us to potential ways in which this Old Testament narrative will anticipate the role and work of Jesus Christ for needy and broken people?

THEOLOGY CONNECTIONS

14. As we saw in the book of Esther, God's hidden hand is obvious at key points in this narrative. Ruth takes the initiative to glean; God leads her to the field of the man who will become a redeemer. What are some other ways, in these first two chapters of Ruth, that you have observed the interplay between the sovereignty of God and real human responsibility?

15. Question 23 of the Westminster Shorter Catechism tells us that Jesus Christ, "as our Redeemer, executeth the offices of a prophet, of a priest, and of a king, both in his estate of humiliation and exaltation." How does Ruth 2 begin to hint at the role that Boaz will have in the redemption of Naomi and Ruth? In what ways is Boaz a Christlike figure, even at this point in the narrative?

APPLYING THE TEXT

16. Boaz obviously stands for God and obeys the law in the midst of the sinful period of the judges. How can he inspire us to cling to God's Word, even when many around us reject it? What else can we learn from Boaz—from his words, his actions, and his character?

17. Naomi's softening heart and words seem to coincide with God's covenant faithfulness being revealed to her through the generosity and kindness of this kinsman-redeemer. How can you remind yourself, today, of God's covenant faithfulness to you? In what ways do gospel "reminders" ward off attitudes of bitterness and anger?

18. Naomi and Ruth return to Bethlehem with profound needs—needs for food, protection, shelter, and relationship. How does their profound need provide a picture of our sin, helplessness, and need for God? How might this help you in your own repentance and dependence upon Jesus Christ?

The Deepest Need, pg. 166

What Naomi and Ruth most needed was not simply a redeemer to rescue them from their earthly poverty and danger, nor even a husband for Ruth. Rather, they needed a heavenly Redeemer to rescue them from their sin. The cost for Naomi and Ruth to have their deepest need supplied was for Jesus—the ever-living one—to taste death in their place.

PRAYER PROMPT

After returning to Bethlehem with nothing, Naomi and Ruth now begin to see God's covenant faithfulness and grace to them through the generosity and kindness of Boaz—this "redeemer" from the clan of Elimelech. Today, as you close your study in Ruth 2, begin by confessing to God your sin, need, and helplessness. Then praise him for offering eternal covenant faithfulness through the great Redeemer, who came for sinners at just the right time!

LESSON 12

RUTH'S REDEEMER

Ruth 3:1–18

THE BIG PICTURE

Ruth's first day of gleaning in the fields of Boaz has gone extremely well, to say the least. By God's grace, she landed on the property of a godly and faithful man—a follower of God's law who took special care to protect and provide for a poor, Moabite widow. Now, even bitter Naomi is beginning to see evidence of God's gracious hand reaching into their situation. So, as chapter 3 opens, Naomi decides to encourage Ruth to take yet another step toward Boaz, her kinsman. Her instructions (3:1–5) are dangerous and risky—she instructs Ruth to essentially sneak into Boaz's bedroom and present herself to him. While she does not give Ruth explicit instructions regarding what she should say, Ruth decides to make a straightforward and earnest appeal to Boaz when he sits up, startled, to find her at his feet in the middle of the night. At this moment, this widowed Moabite woman, who is completely vulnerable and helpless, finds yet more grace and provision at the hands of this godly man. Boaz praises her character, which has already become known throughout Bethlehem. He promises to do all that he can to "redeem" her and take her as his wife. But there's a catch: Boaz knows of one kinsman who is even closer to Naomi's family than he is. The chapter ends with cautious hope, as Naomi and Ruth wait and watch Boaz now springing into action.

Read Ruth 3:1–18.

GETTING STARTED

1. Discuss a time when you took a big risk in the pursuit of something valuable. What did you risk—reputation, respect, money, a relationship? What made the risk seem worthwhile to you?

2. What can hinder us from fully entrusting ourselves to the people around us? How can that hesitancy bleed into our relationship with God? What holds us back from trusting him freely, fully, and without fear?

A Delicate Proposal, pgs. 169–70

Boaz was a man of character (Ruth 2:1). He was a relative of Naomi. He was a man who had already shown himself willing to make costly provision for the poor and the needy. Indeed, the reference to him as "a close relative of ours, one of our redeemers" . . . may already have started Naomi's mind moving in the direction of Boaz's marriage potential as a solution to all of their problems. But how exactly could a woman make such a delicate proposal?

OBSERVING THE TEXT

3. Chapter 2 began with Ruth taking the initiative, but now it is Naomi who springs into action with a plan at the beginning of chapter 3. How are you continuing to witness change in Naomi's actions and words? What seems to be changing in her heart?

4. What is surprising to you in this passage? What aspects of this part of the story might have been deemed "inappropriate" in ancient Israel—and perhaps even in our culture today?

5. How does the chapter conclude? What questions remain for the reader about Naomi and Ruth's fate?

UNDERSTANDING THE TEXT

6. What does Naomi hope will be the result of her plan and instructions for Ruth (3:1–5)? What is she counting on, with regard to the character and integrity of Boaz?

7. What risks are involved for Ruth as she follows Naomi's instructions? What makes this midnight encounter such a vulnerable and dangerous situation for her—especially as a widowed, Moabite woman?

8. What do you notice about Ruth's statement to Boaz in 3:9? Had Naomi instructed her to be this direct? What might Ruth be seeking to avoid, in terms of Boaz's understanding of her intentions?

9. How does Boaz's response to Ruth continue to reveal to us his character (3:10)? What "kindness" does Boaz refer to here? What does he promise to do for Ruth in response to her intentional appeal?

10. According to Boaz's words, does he himself have any legal obligation to marry Ruth and become her kinsman-redeemer? Why does this make his kindness and generosity even more noteworthy? How does this again point us to the Christlike qualities of Boaz and remind us of the generous grace of our Redeemer?

11. As the chapter concludes, Ruth returns to Naomi with a large bundle of barley as they wait together for Boaz to take action. Describe the transformation that has occurred in Naomi and Ruth's situation. What has changed? How has God proved to be faithful?

BIBLE CONNECTIONS

12. Think back to your study of the book of Esther—particularly to her bold request before King Ahasuerus in chapter 7. What similarities do you observe between the risks that both Esther and Ruth took? How would you compare and contrast their motivations for taking these risks?

13. Boaz's gentle and caring response to Ruth points us forward to the gentle care of Jesus for a certain woman in need who approached him. Read Luke 8:43–48. How does Boaz's response to Ruth resemble Jesus's response to the woman of Luke 8?

THEOLOGY CONNECTIONS

14. The doctrine of "total depravity" points us toward an understanding of the radical sinfulness of every human being. We are not all as bad as we could possibly be, but every part of our being is in some way tainted

by sin; we are ultimately helpless to choose God or to save ourselves, unless he acts to save us. How might Ruth's vulnerable and helpless appeal before Boaz present a picture of our utter helplessness before God?

15. Question 15 of the Heidelberg Catechism reminds us that we need a Redeemer who is both fully divine and fully human—"one who is a true and righteous man, and yet more powerful than all creatures; that is, one who is withal true God." Why is this reality about our Redeemer necessary for our salvation? How can Boaz's power and authority—and also his grace and love—give us a glimpse of our divine Redeemer?

APPLYING THE TEXT

16. Think of the tremendous risk that Ruth took as she placed herself at Boaz's feet in the middle of the night! How can her courage embolden you to risk reputation, comfort, and even relationships for the sake of obedience to God's Word and witness for the gospel of Jesus Christ?

> **Who Can We Reach?, pg. 177**
> Naomi was among the undeserving, but because Ruth and Boaz treated her with grace, she came to know the joy of God's salvation. Who are the people that we can reach for Christ, if only we will take a personal risk with the gospel?

17. Naomi continues to be surprised at the grace of God, as her embittered heart continues to thaw. How might this story of Ruth help you to care for people in your life who are embittered, angry, or frustrated with God?

18. We are amazed at Ruth's love and commitment to Naomi and at Boaz's tender and gracious care for Ruth. How should the love that emanates from this narrative expand our understanding of God's loving heart for us, in Christ?

PRAYER PROMPT

In Ruth 3, we have seen how Ruth's tremendous risk is met with gracious kindness from a worthy man, who "will not rest" until her situation is addressed. Today, as you end your study of this passage, spend time thanking God for his gracious provision for you—a helpless sinner—in your redemption through Jesus Christ. Pray, too, that you would be able to follow in the path of Naomi, whose bitterness and anger begin to melt away because of the loving loyalty of Ruth and the gracious kindness of Boaz. Ask God to fill your heart with gratitude for his love and grace, which have been demonstrated most fully at the cross of his Son.

The Real Love Story, pg. 178
The real love story in this book is not about Boaz and Ruth, though. The real love story is behind the scenes. It is the love of God for his straying sheep. It is the love that prevented him from simply ending the world when Adam and Eve first sinned. . . . This love took its fullest shape in the coming of Jesus Christ.

LESSON 13

RUTH'S REWARD

Ruth 4:1–22

THE BIG PICTURE

As Ruth 3 concluded, we were left with a bit of a surprising twist: Naomi has a relative who is a closer kinsman than Boaz is. It looks as if some kind of redemption will come for Naomi and Ruth, no matter what—but it is now unclear whether Boaz will be the one to bring it. Chapter 4 opens with a scene at the "gate" of the town—the usual gathering place for the elders to discuss business matters. Boaz lays out the situation before Naomi's kinsman, who is, very intentionally, never named by the narrator. Initially intrigued by the prospect of adding a field to his possessions, this nameless kinsman quickly backs away after discovering that a Moabite wife will be part of the deal—such a marriage could potentially damage the amount of his inheritance that would go to his current children. So Boaz, again demonstrating his integrity, offers to take Naomi's field, along with Ruth as his wife. The narrative closes with the blessings of the elders of the town falling on Boaz—a kinsman-redeemer for both Naomi and Ruth. But the story does not end there! The final verses of the book of Ruth pan out to show us the bigger perspective on all of this. God has not only been faithful to Naomi and Ruth; he has been faithful to the entire community of Israel. God blesses Boaz and Ruth with a son, whose descendant will be King David. The redemption that takes place in this narrative is part of God's even greater redemption of Israel—and of his church through King David's greater Son.

Read Ruth 4:1–22.

GETTING STARTED

1. Discuss an instance when you became so focused on the minute details of a situation that you lost the bigger perspective. Why is it so important to keep things "in perspective"?

2. Why is it so tempting to evaluate opportunities for helping others based on selfish motives? When have you had someone help you or serve you at great personal cost to themselves? What was your response?

A Final Plot Twist, pgs. 180–81

The narrator also has another plot twist to spring on us at the very end of the book. With a wave of his hand, he reveals to us at the very end that the story has not just been about God providing a solution for the needs of certain individuals. No, in the process, God is also paving the way for the king that his people need.

OBSERVING THE TEXT

3. What questions were we left with at the close of chapter 3? What still needs to happen in order for both Ruth and Naomi to experience healing, fullness, and redemption?

4. Upon your initial reading of Ruth 4, how did you see the character of Boaz continuing to be developed? How is he more fully revealed as a Christlike "redeemer"—selfless, generous, and full of integrity?

5. How does the chapter—and the book of Ruth—conclude? Why might this have been surprising to the original Jewish readers or hearers of this story? Why is the conclusion so significant to an understanding of the deeper meaning of Ruth's story?

UNDERSTANDING THE TEXT

6. The closer kinsman with whom Boaz interacts at the gate of the town is never named (4:1). Why might this be? What is the narrator seeking to communicate to us about this man—and about Boaz?

7. Why might the unnamed kinsman of Naomi have rejected his role as "redeemer" after learning about Ruth? What seems to be his motivation, given his conversation with Boaz? How is Boaz strikingly different from him?

8. What do you observe about Boaz's speech that summarizes his commitment to Naomi's family and to Ruth (4:9–10)? What is he most concerned about? How do the elders of the town respond to his actions and words (4:11–12)?

Legacies, pg. 182
Mr. So-and-So ended up leaving himself nameless, missing out on having a share in the biggest legacy of all: a place in God's plan of salvation. Boaz took a different and more sacrificial approach, embracing the opportunity to leave a legacy for someone else.

9. For only the second time in the book of Ruth, the narrator describes God acting directly, saying that he gave a son to Ruth (4:13). Why is this so significant? How is this a picture of God's surprising redemption?

10. The final verses of the book of Ruth show us the larger perspective—this is not a "random" story, but one that is integrally connected to God's plan to one day provide a great king for his people (4:18–22). What do we learn about the sovereignty and providence of God through this conclusion? How is Ruth's story—and her ethnicity—significant for helping us to understand God's redemptive plan for his people?

11. What are some ways in which the entire story of Ruth displays the gospel of Jesus Christ? Describe and explain the several themes throughout this narrative that teach us about God's grace, his redemption, his mercy toward sinners, and his concern for the poor.

BIBLE CONNECTIONS

12. Hundreds of years after Ruth lived and died, Matthew includes her as one of just five women who are mentioned in the genealogy of Jesus Christ, which begins his gospel. Look at Matthew 1:1–17. Who are

the other women mentioned in Matthew's genealogy of Jesus Christ? What might he be wanting his readers to notice about God's plan?

13. As we have mentioned already, Boaz's redemption of Ruth points us forward to a far greater Redeemer. Read Romans 3:21–26, which is perhaps the theological center of Paul's rich epistle to the Romans. What aspects of the gospel are foreshadowed in the actions, redemption, and grace of Boaz for Ruth and Naomi?

THEOLOGY CONNECTIONS

14. Question 30 of the Westminster Shorter Catechism points us to the application of Christ's redemption to us as believers: "The Spirit applies to us the redemption purchased by Christ, by working faith in us, and thereby uniting us to Christ in our effectual calling." How does the story of Ruth point us toward this glorious reality? In what ways does the marital union of Boaz and Ruth show us the beauty and reality of our union with Christ, our Redeemer?

15. Think back over your entire study of the book of Ruth. In what ways does this narrative expand your view of God's sovereignty and providence? How does this story illustrate sin, need, and human helplessness

before God? In what ways does the book of Ruth teach us about God's gracious and unmerited favor toward sinners in need?

APPLYING THE TEXT

16. How might you, like Boaz, seek to serve others more fully and generously—even at great personal cost to yourself? What often keeps you from doing this?

17. How does the genealogy that concludes this story teach you about the character and plan of God? How might this help you understand your own story in light of God's bigger purposes?

Our Own Stories of Salvation, pg. 192

This is also what the Lord has done for each of us. He is the Redeemer behind each of our own personal salvation stories. He sought each of us while we were utterly lost. Not only did he make us *feel* valuable; in Christ, God actually made us valuable. . . . Your story and my story are also woven into the bigger tapestry of what God is doing in Jesus Christ.

18. When you find yourself, as a sinner, identifying with Ruth and Naomi (being needy, helpless, broken, and so on), how can this narrative help you to celebrate the work of Jesus your Redeemer more fully? What aspects of your own salvation do you understand more fully through your study of the book of Ruth?

PRAYER PROMPT

As you close your study of the book of Ruth, there are good opportunities for you to step back and see this story from a larger perspective. Begin by thanking God for what he reveals about himself through his faithfulness to Naomi and Ruth; praise him for bringing redemption, healing, and fullness to two women in great need. Then thank God for his faithfulness to his people Israel; praise him for sovereignly orchestrating the lineage of King David—a man after his own heart. Finally, thank God that this story of Ruth points us to the greatest redemption that we, as sinners, can know through Jesus Christ; praise him for the great Redeemer, to whom both Boaz and King David point!

Jon Nielson is senior pastor of Spring Valley Presbyterian Church in Roselle, Illinois, and the author of *Bible Study: A Student's Guide*, among other books. He has served in pastoral positions at Holy Trinity Church, Chicago, and College Church, Wheaton, Illinois, and as director of training for the Charles Simeon Trust.

Iain M. Duguid (PhD, University of Cambridge) is professor of Old Testament at Westminster Theological Seminary in Philadelphia. He has written numerous works of biblical exposition, including *Daniel* in the Reformed Expository Commentary series, *Ezekiel* in the NIV Application Commentary series, and *Numbers* in the Preaching the Word series.

Did you enjoy this Bible study? Consider writing a review online. The authors appreciate your feedback!

Or write to P&R at editorial@prpbooks.com with your comments. We'd love to hear from you.

P&R PUBLISHING'S COMPANION COMMENTARY

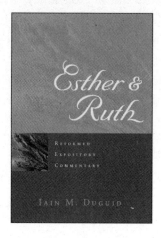

In Esther, God works in invisible ways to save his people. In Ruth, God's grace comes to Naomi unexpectedly, and with it, a depiction of redemption for her people. In both books, a gracious and sovereign God works through flawed individuals—unable even to help themselves—to rescue his people and prepare for the coming of Christ.

The Reformed Expository Commentary (REC) series is accessible to both pastors and lay readers. Each volume in the series provides exposition that gives careful attention to the biblical text, is doctrinally Reformed, focuses on Christ through the lens of redemptive history, and applies the Bible to our contemporary setting.

Praise for the Reformed Expository Commentary Series

"Well-researched and well-reasoned, practical and pastoral, shrewd, solid, and searching." —**J. I. Packer**

"A rare combination of biblical insight, theological substance, and pastoral application." —**Al Mohler**

"Here, rigorous expository methodology, nuanced biblical theology, and pastoral passion combine." —**R. Kent Hughes**